ISLINGTON

Please return this item on or before the last date stamped below or you may be liable to overdue charges. To renew an item call the number below, or access the online catalogue at www.islington.gov.uk/libraries. You will need your library membership number and PIN number.

11/15		

Islington Libraries

020 7527 6900   www.islington.gov.uk/libraries

NIALL HORAN
LOUIS TOMLINSON
LIAM PAYNE
HARRY STYLES

ONE DIRECTION

THE OFFICIAL ANNUAL 2016

Modest!

One Direction are represented exclusively by Richard Griffiths,
Harry Magee and Will Bloomfield for Modest! Management.

ISBN: 978-0-00-814240-7

1 3 5 7 9 10 8 6 4 2

First published in the UK by HarperCollins Children's Books in 2015

All photos taken by Calvin Aurand, One Direction's official photographer
All other images used under licence from Shutterstock
Text by Mandy Archer and Steph Clarkson
Design by Wayne Redwood
Production by Anna Mitchelmore

Quotations taken from: p10 E! Online, Sugarscape, p12 Guardian, p14 Mirror, p16 Sun, Guardian,
pp20/21 Maximum Pop!, 4Music, p27 Capital FM, p39 4Music, p54/55 Sun, The Late Late Show,
BBC Radio 1, The Jonathan Ross Show, MetroLyrics, p57 Billboard

While every effort has been made to trace the owners of copyright material reproduced herein
and secure permissions, the publishers would like to apologise for any omissions and will be
pleased to incorporate missing acknowledgements in any future edition of this book.

HarperCollins *Children's Books*

CONTEN

TS

THE 1D EFFECT

ONE DIRECTION ANNUAL 2016

Following One Direction is like being on a roller coaster – fun, exhilarating and surprising all at the same time! The band don't stand still for a moment, storming up the charts, wowing stadiums and smashing industry records without even breaking a sweat.

Ever since they first bonded on The X Factor, the boys have been on a unique path to superstardom. It's no wonder that they're known for being such hard-working musicians. As soon as a new video is released or a string of tour dates is announced, the fans come out clamouring for more!

So what is 1D's secret? It's something that can't be bottled or explained. Everything about the band is constantly evolving – from their sound to their style. Five years in and One Direction are still on the trip of their life. The good news? You're invited along for the ride...

THE REAL DEAL ON...

We're all wild about Harry. Here's the low-down on Mr Styles...

Name:	Harry Edward Styles
Born:	1 February 1994
Hometown:	Holmes Chapel, Cheshire, England
Star sign:	Aquarius
Height:	5 feet 10 inches (1.78 metres)
Significant others:	Parents Des Styles and Anne Twist, sister Gemma
Musical likes:	Elvis Presley, The Beatles, Coldplay
Hidden talents:	Juggling and playing the kazoo
Fascinating fact:	Harry has somniloquy – he talks in his sleep

Harry gets real on...

...music
"That's the amazing thing about music – there's a song for every emotion. Can you imagine a world where there was no music? It would suck."

...life
"I got told a motto to live by and I've kinda tried it – 'work hard, play hard, be nice'."

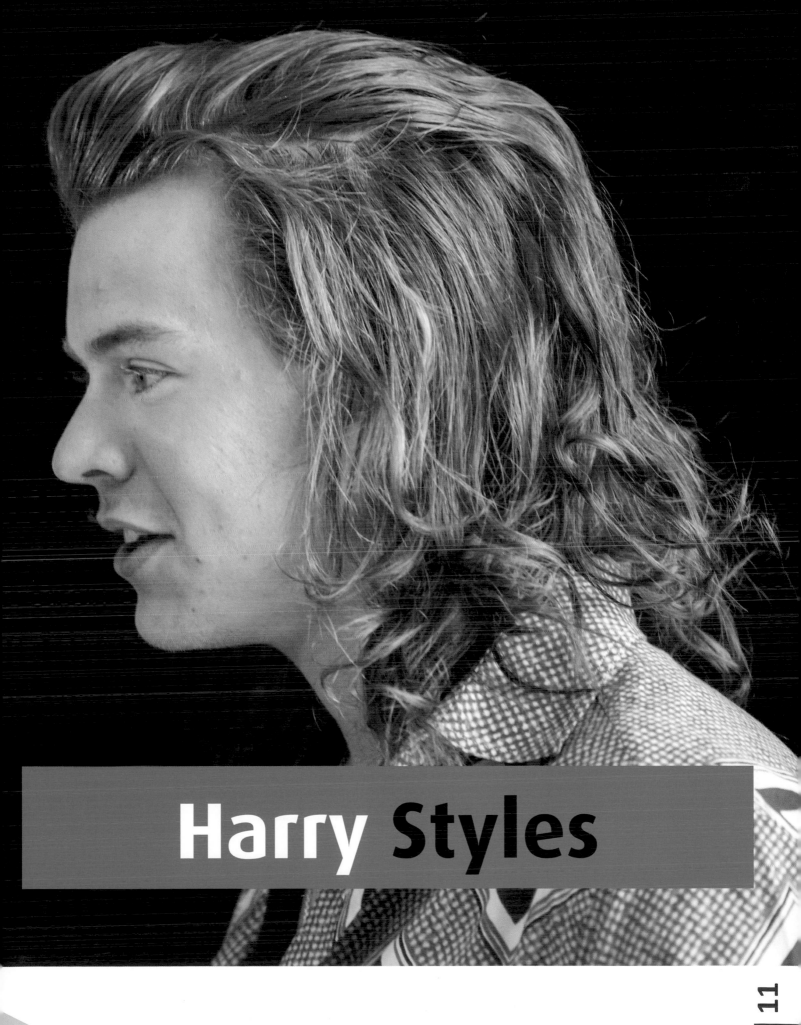

Harry Styles

THE REAL DEAL ON...

Name:	Louis William Tomlinson
Born:	24 December 1991
Hometown:	Doncaster, South Yorkshire, England
Star sign:	Capricorn
Height:	5 feet 9 inches (1.75 metres)
Significant others:	Parents Troy Austin and Johannah Poulston, six half-sisters and a half-brother
Musical likes:	Robbie Williams, Ed Sheeran, The Fray, The Killers
Hidden talents:	Plays piano. Does a mean rendition of The Fray's "How To Save A Life"
Fascinating fact:	Louis is pals with TV star James Corden

Louis gets real on...

...determination
"If you want to do something, go for it – you've got nothing to lose."

...fan loyalty
"It's incredible to have people show their support when you're doing something you love."

Louis Tomlinson

THE REAL DEAL ON...

There's no one like Niall. Here's your chance to swot up on his stats...

Name:	Niall James Horan
Born:	13 September 1993
Hometown:	Mullingar, County Westmeath, Ireland
Star sign:	Virgo
Height:	5 feet 7 inches (1.70 metres)
Significant others:	Parents Bobby Horan and Maura Gallagher, brother Greg
Musical likes:	Eagles, Bon Jovi, Michael Bublé
Hidden talents:	Baking. His dad says he makes the best cupcakes ever
Fascinating fact:	Unlike the rest of the band, Niall has no tattoos – he's not a fan of needles

Niall gets real on...

...creativity
"I guess you might think when we're not on stage we'd want a rest from it (music) but the quiet time is when I get most creative."

...dating
"I'm an emotional guy, so I don't have to worry about a girl trying to get me to open up."

Niall Horan

THE REAL DEAL ON...

Name:	Liam James Payne
Born:	29 August 1993
Hometown:	Wolverhampton, West Midlands, England
Star sign:	Virgo
Height:	5 feet 10 inches (1.78 metres)
Significant others:	Parents Geoff and Karen Payne, sisters Nicola and Ruth
Musical likes:	Pharrell, Kanye West, Passenger
Hidden talents:	Beatboxing – Justin Timberlake taught him
Fascinating fact:	Liam has a phobia of spoons. Yes, really!

Liam gets real on...

...songwriting
"Learning how to write is something I've loved. I love the process – being in the studio feels very natural to me."

...living the dream
"I smile and think, 'This is my job, this is what I do for a living, and it's what I've always wanted.'"

Liam Payne

LET'S GET LYRICAL

ACROSS

1. Baby you light up my world like _ _ _ _ _ _ else
What Makes You Beautiful

4. Can we _ _ _ _ , one more time?
Stop the tape and rewind
Gotta Be You

5. Written on these walls are the _ _ _ _ _ _ _ that I can't change
Leave my heart open but it stays right here in its cage
Story Of My Life

8. Wherever you are is the _ _ _ _ _ I belong
Cos I wanna be free and I wanna be young
Ready to Run

10. Yeah, so tell me girl if every time we...
_ _ _ _ _ , you get this kinda rush
Kiss You

12. Shot me out of the sky
You're my
_ _ _ _ _ _ _ _ _
One Thing

DOWN

2. Couple _ _ _ _ _ _ _ in the whole wide world
Find another one cos she belongs to me
Steal My Girl

3. You can't go to bed without a cup of tea
And maybe that's the reason that you talk in your

_ _ _ _ _
Little Things

6. _ _ _ _ _ _ _ come with the pain that you're running from
Love was something you never heard enough
Where Do Broken Hearts Go

7. Said her name was Georgia Rose
And her daddy was a

_ _ _ _ _ _ _ _
Best Song Ever

9. Seconds and _ _ _ _ _
Maybe they had to take some time
You & I

11. Going out tonight, changes into something _ _ _
Her mother doesn't like that kind of dress
Night Changes

Got 1D tunes lined up on your playlist 24/7? It's time to put your musical mastery to the test! Read the song clues then write the missing lyrics into the crossword grid.

1 NOBODY
2 BILLION (down)
3 SLEEP (down)
4 FALL (down)
5 COLOURS
6 SHADOWS (down)
7 DENTIST (down)
8 PLACE
9 HOURS (down)
10 TOUCH
11 RED (down)
12 KRYPTONITE

VIDEO STARS: STEAL MY GIRL

As well as showcasing an awesome pop anthem, the "Steal My Girl" music video is a feast for the eyes. One Direction emerge from a retro Airstream caravan and ask themselves who the director of their new video might be. Then a car pulls up and the Hollywood legend Danny DeVito steps out, pint-sized in black silk PJs. The boys are all attention as he delivers a motivational speech... "Gentlemen, why are we here? We're here in the name of art; we're here to commit ourselves to a higher form of expression."

As the camera rolls, the desert springs into life...

The location
Vasquez Rocks Natural Area Park, California. The park was chosen for its remote setting and the incredible rock formations exposed by the San Andreas Fault. It has featured heavily in film and TV, most notably in the *Star Trek* TV series.

The directors
The Cirque-du-Soleil-style music video was the brainchild of brothers and directing hotshots Ben and Gabe Turner of Fulwell 73 Productions. Just before the video clip's release, producer Ben Winston warned fans, "You should expect the unexpected on this one. It's weird and wonderful."

The cast
Surely the most varied cast ever to grace the screen in the same video. Masai warriors, sumo wrestlers, ballerinas, a marching band, wild animals (including a lion and flamingos) all played their part in creating the extravaganza. There were even rhythmic gymnasts, a mime artist, a hula-hooper and a man on a penny-farthing!

The props
The props department went wild on this shoot, sourcing everything from a lip-shaped sofa to huge stone-effect hands, a massive birdcage for Liam to stand on and loads of coloured helium balloons.

The lads
What did the boys think of this crazy romp? Here are just some of their on-set and post-vid thoughts...

"I've only been here an hour. I've seen a lion, a bunch of ballerinas and ten Masai warriors – and I'm dressed like this..."
Niall

"It's very warm; I'm wearing a coat; nobody knows why."
Harry

"It's like a dream for me, this... I think I'm going to stay stuck to him [Eli the chimp] all day – or I'm going to try to, anyway."
Louis

"Danny DeVito was not harmed during the filming of the video."
Harry

"That was ridiculous. They made it rain in the desert!"
Niall

"I actually really liked the 'Steal My Girl' video... It was nice and relaxed."
Liam

"It's about an artist who's meant to be the greatest artist of his generation and he's come to shoot a video with us and he wants to do something outside the box, so he's brought us out to the desert to make some crazy images. So I'm, like... the king of the marching band."
Liam

The highlights

• Niall's tribal dancing mixed with the odd contemporary move.

• Danny DeVito's hilarious one-liners.

• Louis' tender handholding with Eli the chimp.

• The rainstorm finale. It's impossible not to smile watching the crazy, free-spirited dance-off.

THE 1D FAMILY

Louis, Niall, Harry and Liam are all adamant about it – without the fans there would be no One Direction. The band say that their fans are the best in the world, bar none. Whenever they can, the lads make time to share a hug, sign autographs or tweet the love. So what makes One Direction fans better than the rest?

Playlist perfection

For you it is, and always has been, about the music. A true fan won't just tell you the name of a song – they'll go on to sing every lyric and tell you which band member is providing the harmonies.

Write and recite

When it comes to 1D, your imagination knows no bounds! The band inspires you to compose songs and draw portraits. You're cool and creative – just like your favourite artists.

Party rock

One Direction gigs are world class and a mega-decibel roar of excitement rises up whenever the band appear on stage. Whether it's rocking out in a giant stadium or dancing to *Four* in your bedroom, you know how to have a good time!

You're a walking 1D Wikipedia

When it comes to dates, facts and figures, One Direction fans always do their homework. You know it all, from fave football teams and funny tour stories, to the lads' star signs!

You love being part of a community

Loving One Direction is infectious! The instant that you started following the band, you became part of a massive global network of like-minded people. The web is full of places for you to share the love – on forums, through the fan club and on social media.

Your loyalty knows no bounds

Many of us have been fans since the beginning, way back in those early X-Factor days. But whether you're an old or a new fan, your allegiance is never in question. You wear the T-shirts, cover your room in posters and talk to your mates about them all the time.

You know that you're special

Being a fan of One Direction is a two-way street – Harry, Liam, Niall and Louis love you just as much as you love them! It's a relationship that the boys treasure and talk about all the time. In March 2015, Liam said, "For the past five years now I've been part of something so special I don't think any of us really understand, something that can mean the world to people and put a smile on the face of our fans even in the darkest times."

A YEAR IN THE LIFE

One Direction spend so much time travelling the world to entertain us, it's a wonder they get to do anything off-stage at all! Luckily for us, they're uber-hardworking. Here's a snapshot of their antics over the last year.

• The back end of 2014 saw the boys busy with the release of their album *Four* and the first two singles, "Steal My Girl" and "Night Changes".

• In November 2014, the band performed "Night Changes" on the railway bridge of the set of *Eastenders* as part of the Children in Need appeal. The performance helped the charity to raise over £32 million.

• The boys kicked off 2015 with a slot on the US show *Dick Clark's New Year's Rockin' Eve*, performing a medley of their biggest hits to an audience in LA.

• When the BRITs 2015 nominations were announced in January, unsurprisingly, the boys were up for British Group, and British Video for "You & I".

• Before jetting off for the Australian leg of the band's world tour, Liam attended the NBA Global Games at London's 02 Arena. He got to see a top basketball match – the New York Knicks vs the Milwaukee Bucks.

• Niall, meanwhile, spent a few days in Melbourne, watching Andy Murray and co thrash it out in the Australian Open.

• In February 2015, the boys popped up on YouTube in an ad for pal James Corden's new US chat show, *The Late Late Show*.

• At the BRITs in February, Simon Cowell took to the stage to pick up the British Video award on behalf of the boys, who were (you guessed it!) touring.

• At the beginning of March, the lads came home to Blighty. Harry treated his mum to dinner at a wine bar in Knutsford, while Louis was a judge at the Syco and Sony Music *Be in the Band* girl group auditions in London.

- The boys made a snap appearance on *Comic Relief* (by video from South East Asia) to introduce "the greatest One Direction tribute band of all time". The aptly named "No Direction" starred Johnny Vegas as Liam, Patrick Kielty as Niall, Vic Reeves as Harry and Jack Dee as Louis.

- Huge-hearted Harry took time out of the South-African leg of the tour to visit underprivileged children being helped by Cape Town's Lalela Project.

- In early April 2015, keen golfer Niall earned his stripes as a caddie by lugging Rory McIlroy's golf bag around at the Masters Par 3 competition at Augusta in the US.

- In April, the lads also released their new-look *On The Road Again* tour poster.

- Intrepid Liam and Harry found five minutes to trek up Machu Picchu in Peru, trailed by hordes of photographers and fans.

- In the spring of 2015, Liam, Louis, Harry and Niall returned to the studio to work on their fifth album. The boys posted pics of themselves with musicians such as Juicy J and Nickelback's Chad Kroeger. Liam said that the recording was going, "really well," adding, "The songs have been coming out a bit more chilled. We want this to be an album that you can listen to any time."

- Liam, Louis and Niall put on their finest attire to attend the Great Gatsby Ball at the Bloomsbury Ballroom in April. A trip to meet the boys was one of the prizes on offer in the fundraising auction for the charity Trekstock, with the proceeds helping young people who have cancer.

- Louis had a great time playing in a testimonial match for legendary Doncaster Rovers midfielder James Coppinger.

- Niall managed to get to Stamford Bridge to watch Chelsea beat Crystal Palace, clinching the Premier League title.

- While in the capital, Niall also helped Irish gal Laura Whitmore celebrate her thirtieth birthday, attending her 80s fancy dress party as Tom Cruise in the *Top Gun* movie.

- In June, the band kicked off Capital FM's Summertime Ball.

Q. Where was your last selfie taken?
A. Erm... probs with my sister Lottie.

Q. If you could give an award to one of your fellow band mates, what would it be for?
A. Cutest Irishman Award.

Q. If you weren't in 1D, which band (current or past) would you like to have been part of?
A. That's pretty tough. Maybe The Fray – I've always loved them.

Q. What's your favourite new fashion trend and what would you not be seen dead in?
A. I just love my tour joggers.

Q. What's your most treasured possession?
A. I guess my home. I love having all my friends and family there, hanging out.

Q. Where do you see yourself in ten years' time?
A. I hope we're still touring!

Q. What's the most embarrassing thing that has happened to you?
A. Maybe that awkward thing where when you first meet someone, you go in for a hug, they go for air kisses 'n' you bump in the middle – awful.

Q. What has been your favourite music video to make so far?
A. "Steal My Girl", hands down. It was just chaos.

Q. Is there anything you haven't done yet in your videos that you'd like to?
A. We spend ages thinking of ideas for our videos. Maybe skydiving or something like that.

Q. What do you like about being on tour?
A. Waking up somewhere different every day is pretty cool. We meet loads of people along the way.

Q. Is there any corner of the world you haven't yet visited, but would like to?
A. There's lots of China we still haven't been to.

Q. What three things are always in your suitcase?
A. Laptop, PlayStation, pants.

Q. What's the first thing you do whenever you get home?
A. Have a nice cuppa – proper British tea.

Q. What are your favourite things about the recording process?
A. I love that feeling when there's a few of you in a room, and all of a sudden the vibe starts to come together.

Q. What's your favourite 1D memory from 2015?
A. Touring new places – that's been pretty cool.

Q. How do you stay grounded?
A. Well, the other boys really help that. Then I do have quite a few of my mates who join the tour for a week or two at a time.

Q. What advice would you give to people just starting out in the music industry?
A. Go for it, give it everything you've got and enjoy it.

Q. Finish this sentence: "I would never..."
A. ...lose touch with my family and mates – they're so important to me.

#HELLO, TWEEPS

There's no doubt about it, One Direction are all over Twitter! The guys love to share, post and chat online. With over 86 million followers between them, they're a social-media phenomenon. Here are some of the band's best tweets of 2015. Which is your favourite?

Huge day of writing so excited the team never stop!
Liam

Just learned how to say walkie talkie in French
Harry

Our fans' support really has been a different class! Huge love to you guys!!
Louis

Been on a safari trip for the last couple of days! One of those bucket list things to do, incredible experience
Niall

You can never outgrow Spongebob
Liam

Can't wait for the show tonight! Yesterday was sooooo fun!!
Louis

Scribbling, scribbling.
Harry

Been a crazy couple of days but know that we are going to work harder than ever to deliver the best album we've ever made for you guys!
Louis

Been a mad few days and your support has been incredible as per usual! This in turn spurs us on to make the best music we possibly can
Niall

Sometimes I talk to myself so I guess it's better I do it on here : |
Liam

As far as I'm aware, the doors are open. And we're On The Road Again.
Harry

Another day of writing today, really working hard on this next album. Hope you lot love it!!
Louis

Great few days in the studio this week! Having a really good time writing, playing guitar parts! Exciting times
Niall

Don't know how I'm going to sleep tonight had far too much excitement for one day
Liam

All the love as always. H
Harry

Twitter Storm!

Last year, Harry broke the Internet! His thank you message to fans on the band's fourth anniversary was the most retweeted tweet of 2014. When the fifth came around in April 2015, he didn't forget to post again...

It's been five years. Thank you for all your support so far. Isn't it lovely. H

STYLE FILE

One Direction's music, vibe and style make it clear that they're not your typical boy band. Rather than being coordinated in matchy-matchy outfits, the lads prefer to express their personalities in their own relaxed, laidback way. Their stylist Julie Feingold has watched the band's style mature over the years. Now they have the confidence to pull off loads of new looks, whether it's putting on a smart suit for a movie premiere or rocking out in skinny jeans and retro band tees for a stadium gig.

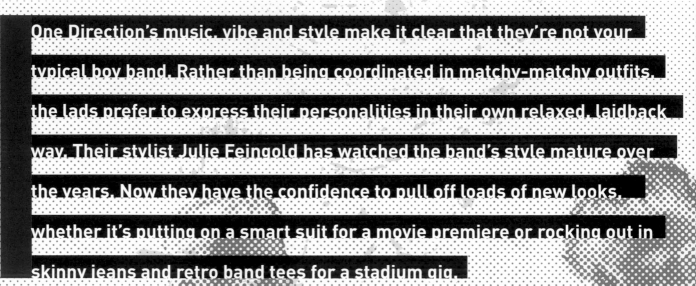

Niall used to favour a no-effort baggy look, but these days his outfits have more of an edge. When he's on stage, look out for simple monochrome tees and bold high-tops. Niall likes to add a touch of sports luxe for premieres and nights out, opting for relaxed flannels and baseball jackets.

Louis is the master of vintage. Classic-label polo shirts, low-waisted chinos and retro brogues all add up to a relaxed, casual style. When he's performing, the star chooses distressed band tees or vests teamed with his favourite skinny jeans – what's not to love?!

Liam is a fashion chameleon. On tour, his wardrobe rail is packed with simple white vests, classic leather jackets and relaxed jeans. After hours, Liam's style is grown-up, manly and confident – blending perfectly with his closely-trimmed beard and understated accessories.

Harry has always had an eclectic boho style, but the emphasis is now less on preppy and more on rock-star cool. On stage and off, our boy likes to wear black, black and black again! But he's not afraid of colour and loves a scarf, an open shirt and a Cuban heel.

FASHION FLOW CHART

Which One Direction band member shares your fashion sense? Let's find out! Work your way across the flow chart, picking the choices that suit you best. Your style icon will be waiting at the end!

neutrals

Bright or neutrals?

brig...

trainers

bold

Quirky or bold?

brogues

quirky

Brogues or trainers?

Tailored or casual?

dress down

START

hat

Dress up or dress down?

tailored

dress up

Scarf or hat?

Pre-loved or brand-new?

brand...

scarf

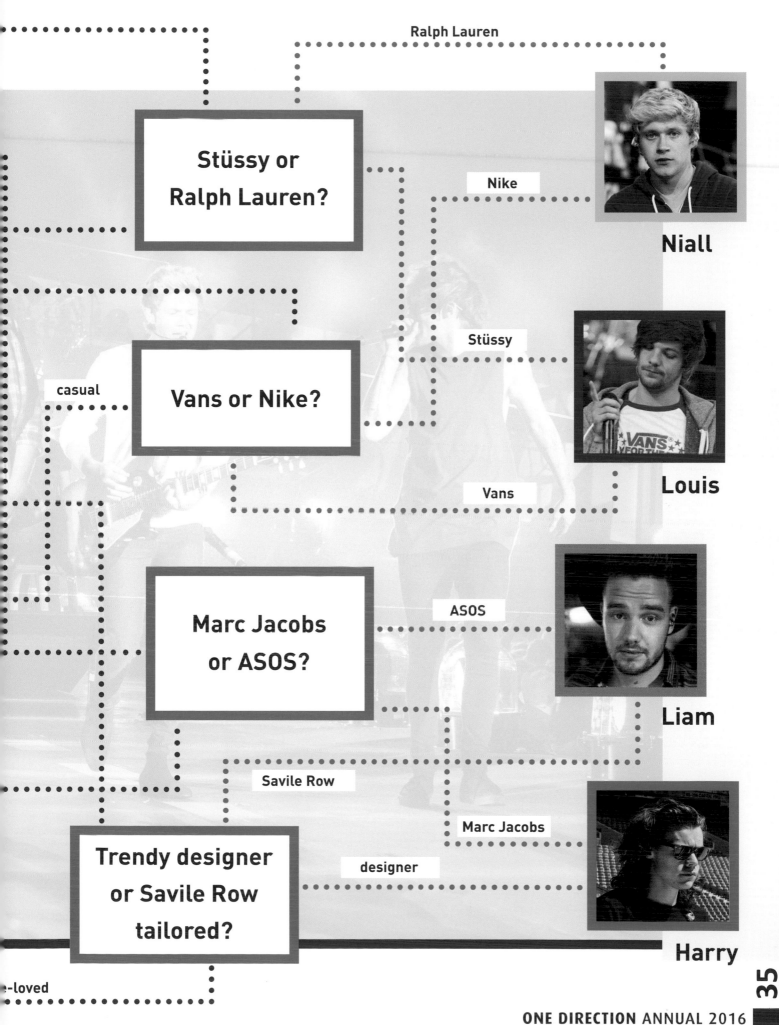

Ralph Lauren

Stüssy or
Ralph Lauren?

Nike

Niall

casual

Stüssy

Vans or Nike?

Louis

Vans

ASOS

Marc Jacobs
or ASOS?

Liam

Savile Row

Marc Jacobs

designer

Trendy designer
or Savile Row
tailored?

Harry

-loved

The blonde, baby-faced lad from

Q. Where was your last selfie taken?
A. Some party, probably.

Q. If you could give an award to one of your band mates, what would it be for?
A. Best Moonwalk – Payno.

Q. If you weren't in 1D, which band (current or past) would you like to have been part of?
A. The Eagles – my favourite band.

Q. What's your favourite new fashion trend and what would you not be seen dead in?
A. I've got a new flat cap that I'm literally wearing every day. It's my fave new thing.

Q. What's the craziest thing a fan has ever given you?
A. We got given a frog once. That was weird.

Q. What's the most embarrassing thing that has happened to you?
A. Falling over on live TV at the Augusta Masters must be up there.

Q. What's your favourite lyric?
A. Your hand fits in mine like it's made just for me.

Q. What has been your favourite music video to make so far?
A. "Steal My Girl" was absolutely bonkers and having the chance to have Danny DeVito, a true Hollywood legend, star in it made it a day I will never forget.

Q. Is there anything you haven't done yet in your videos that you'd like to?
A. Irish dancing.

Q. What do you like about being on tour?
A. Everything. I love gigging, travelling, tour life in general. I could honestly do it for all my life.

Q. Is there any corner of the world you haven't yet visited, but would like to?
A. Fiji.

Q. Where do you see yourself in ten years' time?
A. On the road.

Q. What's the first thing you do whenever you get home?
A. Relax.

Q. What are your favourite things about the recording process?
A. I obviously love writing, but I love playing guitar, and being able to hear myself on the actual album song gives me even more pleasure.

Q. What's your favourite 1D memory from 2015?
A. The safari experience was amazing!

Q. How do you stay grounded?
A. The rest of the band ensure we all stay grounded. Other than that, my family. I live with my older cousin, Willie.

Q. What advice would you give to people just starting out in the music industry?
A. Be yourself and enjoy every minute.

Q. Finish this sentence: "I would never..."
A. ...travel without my guitar.

FOUR

Floored by _Four_? Join the club. The lads' album has floored critics and delighted fans with its edgy pop/rock sound and layered lyrics. If you haven't yet downloaded your copy, there are sooo many reasons why you should...

It has synergy

Niall came up with the name _Four_. "It's our fourth album, we'd been together four years, it just seemed fitting," he says. Harry agrees. "We thought all the previous albums followed a pattern. This album was a bit different, a bit more of a statement, so it made sense to have a bold one-word title."

It's massive

OK, so the disk is still very much the size of a normal CD, but the content is huge! The album features a whopping sixteen tracks. According to the lads, this is because they had so much material to choose from. The band recorded twenty-four songs before deciding on the final tracklist. Niall says, "We had a meeting with Simon, the label and management and everyone. This time round it was a lot easier because we were all on the same page. The songs that made it on all stood out and that's why we made a larger album."

ONE DIRECTION ANNUAL 2016

It's personal

The band put so much of themselves into the making of the record, they found putting it out there pretty nerve-wracking. "We write from personal experience – everybody does," Harry says. "When you've been working on the album all year, it's all built up to that moment when you put it out and everyone hears it. You almost feel vulnerable."

Favourite track on the album

- *Liam* – "Fireproof"

- *Harry* – "Stockholm Syndrome"

- *Louis* – "Fireproof"

- *Niall* – "Where Do Broken Hearts Go"

It's for you

While the band love to receive plaudits for their work, it's the fans that they're really looking to impress. "Of course you care what critics say," Louis admits, "but I like to have a look on Twitter and search different song titles and see what people are saying about them, because ultimately that's the thing that matters – what the fans think of it. It's cool to read a good write-up... but actually we're looking for recognition from the fans."

It's a matter of pride

The boys are proud of their work and it shows in the quality of the songwriting. Liam says this is partly due to having something to prove. "What was amazing about this album was that we were set a really tough challenge, what with it being our fourth album and with the success we had off the back of the last one, and we were all a little bit nervous coming into the writing of it. So the thing we're most proud of is that we stepped up to the mark and the songs just came so quick, thick and fast. Every single day there was a different song that everyone was buzzing about."

It's a departure

This album marks a real change from the last and is miles away from the pop sound of *Up All Night*. "We've taken inspiration from a lot of different places," says Liam. "It's kind of more Fleetwood-Mac-y style... We've gone for those Eagles harmonies."

It's historic

Released globally on 17 November 2014, *Four* hit number one in the album charts in 65 countries on the day it was made available for pre-order. It also made One Direction the first band to debut at the top of the US Billboard charts with their first four albums.

ON THE
ROAD
AGAIN

No artist can make a stadium explode like One Direction! On 7 February 2015, the boys embarked on their fourth headlining concert tour – a mega road trip through six of the globe's seven continents. This time the stakes were higher than ever before. *Where We Are* had been a massive production and the top earning tour of 2014. This time the lads wanted to wow their fans with an even bigger, more-breathtaking concert experience. From the status updates, vines and pics posted by the thousands of fans who turned out to share it, the band did not disappoint…

The action kicked off down under in Sydney, Australia. After a series of knockout gigs, the tour moved on to Asia, South Africa and Dubai. The boys' stunning set list lifted fans to their feet for two hours of fun, excitement and unforgettable music.

After their success in the southern hemisphere, the guys took a spring break to focus on writing their next album. A couple of months later, they were refreshed and ready to climb back on the tour bus. The first UK gigs were at the Millennium Stadium in Cardiff, with McBusted firing up the stage as the support act. After two wild nights in Wales, the band rocked through Europe, North America and back again. The best bit? The band don't even try to keep it a secret. They loved it ALL just as much as the fans did!

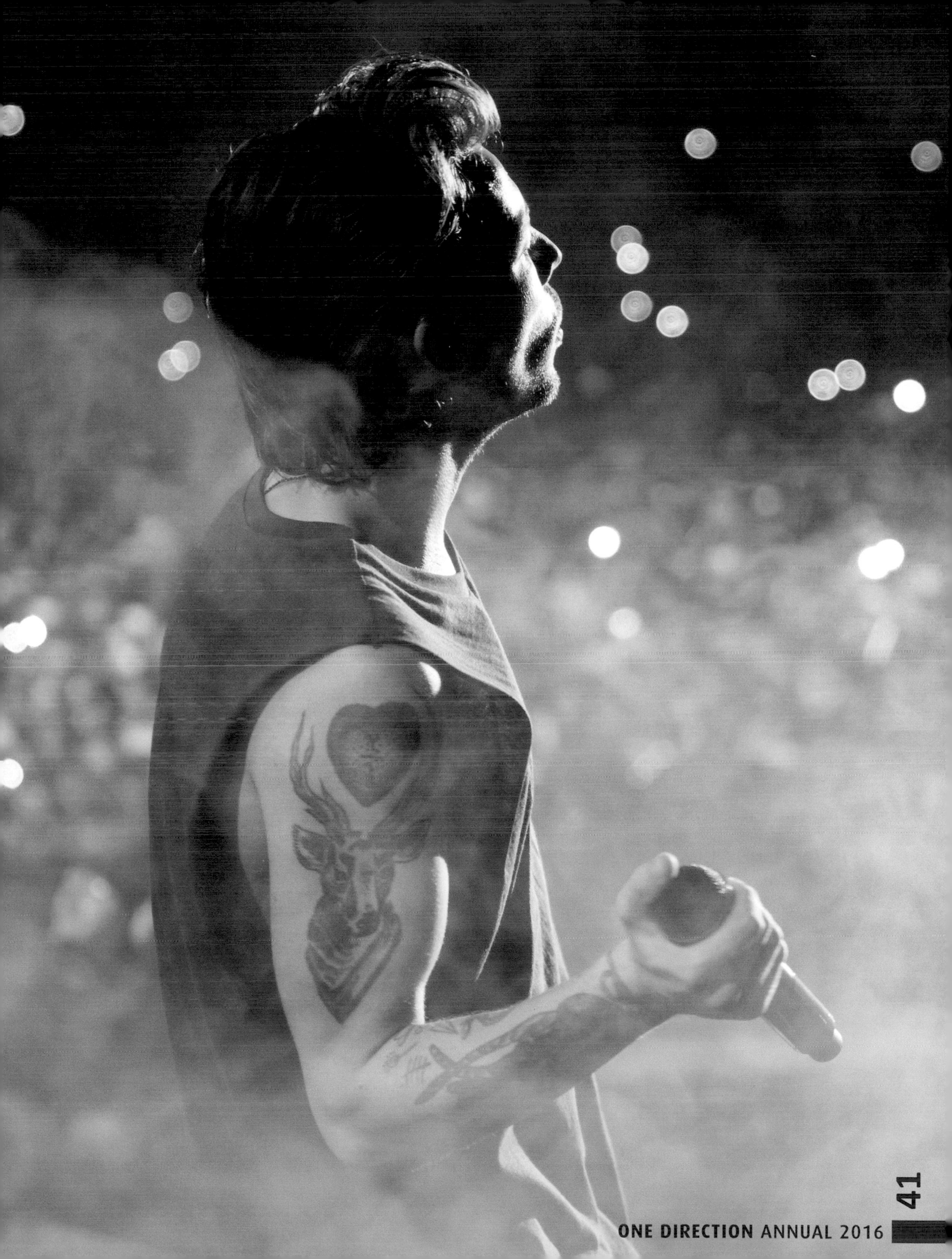

So what's it like at a One Direction gig? If you've not been before, brace yourself – it's an experience that will stay with you for the rest of your life! A crackle of electricity sparks up the instant you step into the venue. Once the party starts, anything can happen...

On The Road Again – the best bits

- Harry, Liam, Niall and Louis rising up on the stage.

- Niall's crazy dancing.

- Lots and lots of fireworks (with some lasers and streamer cannons thrown in).

- The boys bantering on stage. 1D shows aren't scripted – what you see is the real deal!

- Harry's water-spouting thing.

- Unswervingly brilliant vocals and amazing harmonies.

- The best encore ever.

BOYS ON TOUR

Who is as excited as me for this show tonight? Answer = absolutely none of you
Niall

Today was like 1st day at school and u sit at your test paper and everything goes except there's lots of people and I had no pen . . .
. . . but Sydney you were amazing thank you for being a great start to the tour hope we made a few people smile :)
Liam

Johannesburg, you were amazing tonight. I fell in love with you fast. Thank you for coming. H
Harry

The shows have been sooooo good so far!! Love performing the new songs!!!
Louis

Getting back on the road tomorrow. Can't wait to see all of you in Cardiff.
Harry

Can't wait for the show tonight! Yesterday was sooooo fun!!
Louis

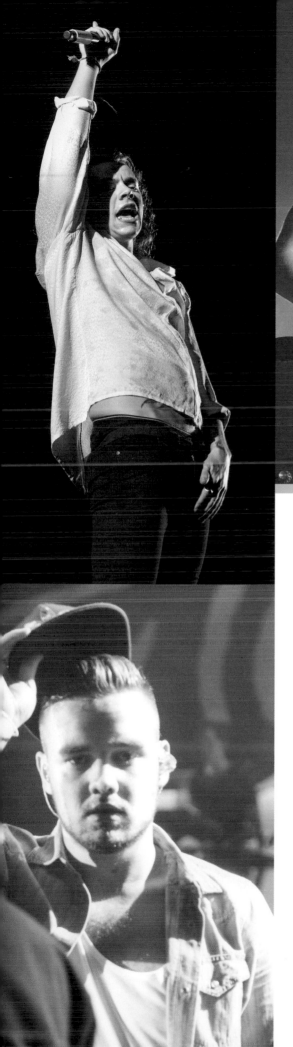

SET LIST

Clouds, Steal My Girl,
Little Black Dress,
Where Do Broken Hearts Go,
Midnight Memories, Kiss You,
Stockholm Syndrome,
Ready To Run, Strong,
Better Than Words,
Don't Forget Where You Belong,
Little Things, Night Changes,
18, Alive, Diana, No Control,
What Makes You Beautiful,
Through The Dark,
Girl Almighty,
Story Of My Life, You & I,
Little White Lies,
Best Song Ever.

Forget the photo shoots –

Q. Where was your last selfie taken?
A. Probably at home, with the dogs!

Q. If you could give an award to one of your band mates, what would it be for?
A. Longest Hair Award – Mr Styles.

Q. What's your worst habit?
A. Love a bit of junk food.

Q. Where do you see yourself in ten years' time?
A. Home, happy, with a family and a dog.

Q. What's the most embarrassing thing that has happened to you?
A. Someone stole my underpants.

Q. What has been your favourite music video to make so far?
A. "Best Song Ever" was so much fun to make. As everyone can clearly see, we aren't the best dancers!

Q. Is there anything you haven't done yet in your videos that you'd like to?
A. Bungee jumping.

Q. What do you like about being on tour?
A. I love performing – I always have. Also meeting our fans and sharing the experience with them is unbelievable.

Q. Is there any corner of the world you haven't yet visited, but would like to?
A. Antarctica

Q. What three things are always in your suitcase?
A. Headphones, passport and underpants.

Q. What's the first thing you do whenever you get home?
A. Lie on my sofa.

Q. What are your favourite things about the recording process?
A. I love heading to a studio to write. Writing music with great writers and producers is a pleasure.

Q. What's your favourite 1D memory from 2015?
A. The shows in South Africa were amazing.

Q. How do you stay grounded?
A. The other boys always keep me grounded. That is something only friends can do.

Q. What advice would you give to people just starting out in the music industry?
A. Try, try and keep trying.

Q. Which motto do you try to live by?
A. Work hard, play hard.

Q. Finish this sentence: "I would never..."
A. ...imagine a world without music.

VIDEO STARS: NIGHT CHANGES

Would you go on a date with 1D? In the "Night Changes" music video, the boys invite you to do just that! The festive hit from the *Four* album showed each of the band members reliving a date with a mystery girl. The mood is set for love and romance, but things don't quite go to plan. Director Ben Winston described the video as "almost like a fantasy sequence… but each date just goes that little bit wrong to show that [the boys] are human after all." Shooting the video wasn't as easy as it looked. The boys had to stare deep-and-meaningfully into a camera lens, trying to act as if it was a real person. Luckily they pulled it off with flying colours!

The dates

Harry
Harry's date is treated to an evening outdoors at the skating rink. As the night unfolds, our boy can't resist showing off his favourite moves. He spins and twirls, then reaches out to lift the camera into the air. It's a stretch too far – Harry and his date are sent crashing onto the ice, hurting his wrist and her ankle in the process. Sad face!

Niall
What could be nicer than a cosy night in? Niall's plan to snuggle up in front of the fire seems harmless enough. He is filmed with board games, a guitar and a cute pet pooch to cuddle. But the date ends in disaster when Niall stokes the fire, sets the arm of his winter woolly alight, then spills his drink all over his date's lap!

Liam

When it comes to a first date, fun is clearly at the top of Liam's list. He is shown having a blast in a fairground. Too much of a blast. After buying toffee apples and trying his luck on the stalls, Liam overdoes it on the waltzer. The car spins round and round making our Romeo so queasy he can't help throwing up in his date's hat. Awkward!

Louis

Normally a smart suit, beautiful scenery and a classic car would be a recipe for dating success, but Louis isn't quite so lucky. Once he gets behind the steering wheel, he can't resist hitting the gas. A policeman appears out of nowhere to promptly arrest Louis for speeding – date over!

The location

This was the first video that the band shot individually. Although they couldn't be together, the boys enjoyed being back in the UK to record the footage. Harry's ice-skating session took place on the rink at the Natural History Museum in London, while Louis shot his segment in Hyde Park.

The highlights

• Louis playing the perfect gent behind the wheel of a vintage Austin Healey motor car.

• The cute pooch with lookie-likie hair snuggled up in Niall's cosy living room.

• Harry giving it his all on the ice, complete with wobbly turns and a disastrous lift! Afterwards he said proudly, "That's method acting, that is!"

• Liam taking selfies and giving up his scarf to keep his date warm.

1D LOTTO

1. Walk the length of a pier on a stormy day.

2. Watch a Doncaster Rovers match on TV or from the terraces.

3. Get up close with some wildlife at a zoo, safari park or on holiday. Don't cross this square off until you've seen a lion, flamingos and a chimpanzee.

4. Visit Ireland or celebrate St Patrick's Day.

5. Make some fan art inspired by your favourite band member.

6. Eat toasted marshmallows around a campfire.

7. Take a city tour on an open-top bus. Make sure you sing your favourite 1D hits while you're doing it.

8. Try a round of golf.

9. Get one of the boys' autographs.

10. Share a hot chocolate and a board game by the fire.

11. Go ice skating. Try not to do a Harry!

12. Eat a toffee apple at the fair then go on the waltzer.

13. Feed the ducks in the park with someone special.

14. Make a collage of old family snaps to see how you've all changed.

15. Practise your "That Moment" face. In the words of Girolle, photographer on the "That Moment" campaign, "sink of zat moment... make ze face of ze smell."

16. Fool your friends with a cunning disguise.

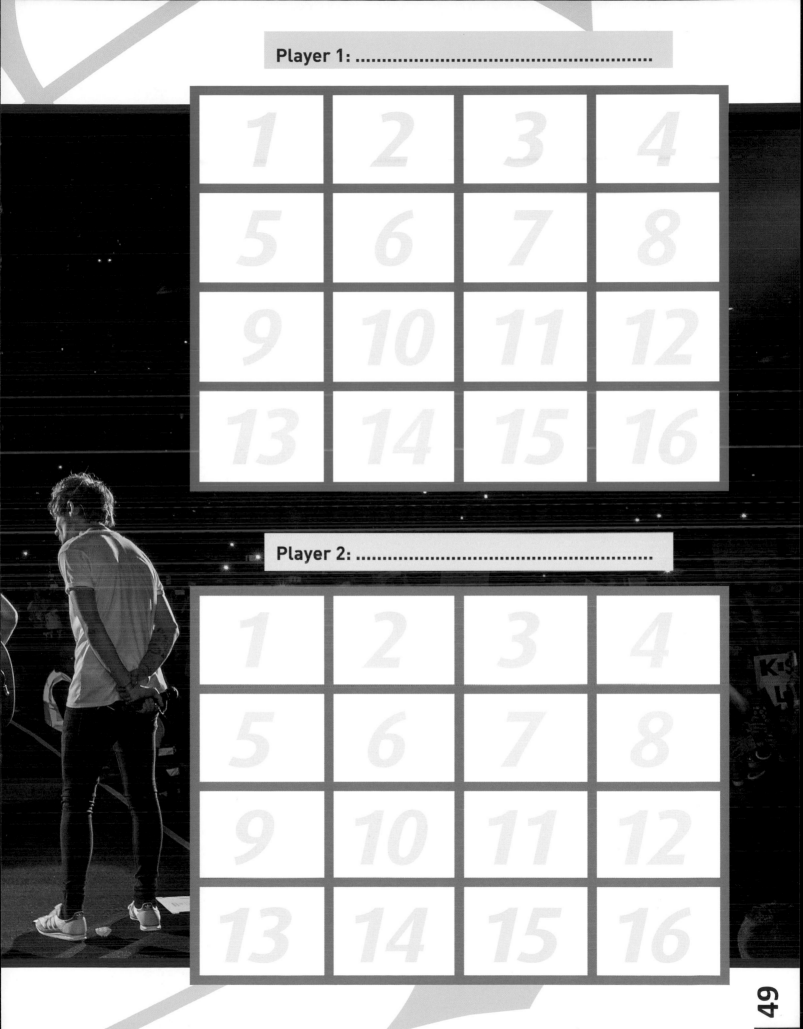

Player 1: ....

1	2	3	4
5	6	7	8
9	10	11	12
13	14	15	16

Player 2: ....

1	2	3	4
5	6	7	8
9	10	11	12
13	14	15	16

It's another amazing interview.

Q. Where was your last selfie taken?
A. I can honestly say I've never taken one.

Q. What's your favourite new fashion trend and what would you not be seen dead in?
A. Oooooh, I do love a beret. Not a big camo fan.

Q. What's the most amazing thing a fan has ever done for you?
A. For my birthday this year some fans gave money to a charity.

Q. What was the last book you read?
A. Keith Richards' autobiography.

Q. What's your most treasured possession?
A. A gift from my dad that I got for my eighteenth birthday.

Q. What's your worst habit?
A. Correcting spelling.

Q. What's the most embarrassing thing that has happened to you?
A. I got caught mooning at an old lady's window when I was four.

Q. What has been your favourite music video to make so far?
A. Probably "What Makes You Beautiful". We had no idea what we were doing. It was just us running around, having fun on a beach.

Q. Is there anything you haven't done yet in your videos that you'd like to?
A. Hang upside down.

Q. What do you like about being on tour?
A. I love travelling and performing so touring is an amazing combination of both those things.

Q. Is there any corner of the world you haven't yet visited, but would like to?
A. Hawaii.

Q. What three things are always in your suitcase?
A. Candle, phone charger, pants.

Q. What's the first thing you do whenever you get home?
A. Go to the fridge.

Q. What is your favourite thing about the recording process?
A. An idea or a whistle or a phrase can become a song on an album. It's fun to be able to be a part of something like that.

Q. What's your favourite 1D memory from 2015?
A. Touring, especially in Asia. Visiting all those new places has been really amazing.

Q. How do you stay grounded?
A. I feel very lucky to have such an amazing support group through my friends and family.

Q. What advice would you give to people just starting out in the music industry?
A. Have fun.

SAY IT LIKE IT IS

They're chatty types, the 1D boys!

"It's very exciting to be working on our fifth album. It shows how incredible the fans have been."
Harry

"In my first video diary I explained my love for women who have a taste in carrots. Since then, I have received plenty of carrots. Now I also have a keen interest in women who like Lamborghinis."
Louis

"I used to have an imaginary friend named Michael."
Niall

"I've always wanted to be one of those people who didn't really care much what people thought about them, but I don't think I am."
Harry

"I've forgotten [lyrics] a couple of times... Sometimes you'll be reading someone's sign and you'll start to sing what's on the sign. Sometimes that's really bad because we get some really fruity signs."
Liam

"A real girl isn't perfect and a perfect girl isn't real."
Harry

"The Story of My Life is drinking cups of tea, eating Coco Pops and playing PlayStation."
Louis

"I love it when people do drawings of us – there's some really good artists out there who spend a lot of time on it."
Liam

"At the VMAs all the artists were sitting around us, drinking beer. Rihanna's behind us with a glass of champagne and we're just sitting there eating foot-long hot dogs. I was like, we are the worst celebrities that ever walked the earth."
Niall

"Have you ever put maple syrup on fried chicken? Sounds random but it's really nice."
Liam

"I grew up with just my mum and sister, so I respect women a lot."
Harry

"I fart all the time... I was a colic child which means I can't burp so everything comes out the other end."
Niall

"I've only ever cooked one meal – that was pretty nice. Chicken, wrapped in Parma ham, stuffed with mozzarella. Winner."
Louis

"I don't think my mum actually saw our film – she was just crying the whole time, as per. She told me she was wearing the 3D glasses and in the end they got fogged up so she couldn't see what was going on."
Liam

"Throw it up. Roll a li'l thing around it. It's just that simple!"
Harry (on achieving the perfect man bun!)

"I think our fans are a bit like us – they're very fun, like to have a laugh, like to party."
Niall

DOWNTIME

When you're so famous you've been around the world more times than you can remember, what do you do to relax? It's not always easy when you can't walk out of the door without getting mobbed. While the rest of us mere mortals want to jet off to exotic climes or pack our downtime with activity, the lads seek out simpler pleasures.

Home is where the heart is

There's nowhere the lads would rather be than at home. They each spend as much of their time off as possible unwinding in their hometowns, seeing friends and family.

Turn on, tune in

All the boys admit to loving screen time. Harry likes watching movies and is not averse to a romcom. He's recently notched up mega-weepies *One Day* starring Anne Hathaway and *The Notebook* featuring Rachel McAdams and Ryan Gosling.

Gamers

While Louis is committed to his PlayStation, Niall also enjoys old-style gaming. Ed Sheeran says that the pair played several games of Monopoly over Christmas.

Snooze-fest

With such tightly-packed and relentless schedules, it's not surprising that the lads crave some time in bed. They all claim that their ideal day off would start with a looong lie-in.

Food, glorious food

Forget dining out in fancy restaurants, when the boys are chillaxing that's the last thing they want to do. Louis and Harry love a home-cooked Sunday roast. Liam enjoys a curry, while Niall just loves food in general. He says that any day off has to revolve around great meals, starting with breakfast in bed.

Football crazy

Like most lads, quality downtime for 1D involves watching the footy... or the rugby... or the boxing... or the darts. When he's not actually on the pitch at Doncaster Rovers, Louis loves a kickabout with his mates. He also heads to the gym for a workout on his days off, finding it a great way to de-stress.

Gone fishing

Liam loves fishing. He takes every opportunity to get out on the open water. While in San Diego, he even managed to catch a baby shark – although he threw it back.

Music

Music isn't just a job for the lads – it's a passion. When they're not plugged in to their iPods, checking out new artists, they're playing instruments. Chilling out with his guitar makes Niall happy. He says, "Someone told me the smile on my face gets bigger when I play the guitar." Liam prefers to head down to the studio to play about with mixing tracks.

IT'S A CRAZY, CRAZY CRAZY WORLD

Life's pretty crazy in 1D World. Can you sort the fact from the fiction here? The answers are below – no peeking!

1. Liam had his pants stolen from his hotel room in Australia.
☐ True
☐ False

2. The boys once sent Simon Cowell a birthday card with money in it – 50p from each band member.
☐ True
☐ False

3. On Graham Norton's chat show, Niall asked to leave the sofa to go for a wee.
☐ True
☐ False

4. The first gig Harry ever attended was Nickelback.
☐ True
☐ False

5. Louis once appeared as an extra in a film starring the Oscar® winner James McAvoy.
☐ True
☐ False

6. Liam's dad originally suggested that the band call themselves USP.
☐ True
☐ False

7. Liam was on the reserve list for sprinting at the London 2012 Olympics before he was in One Direction.
☐ True
☐ False

8. The only book Niall has ever read all the way through is the classic novel *Of Mice and Men*.
☐ True
☐ False

9. Niall hates birds, particularly pigeons, since being attacked while on the toilet.
☐ True
☐ False

10. In May 2012, Liam broke his toe playing football with Louis.
☐ True
☐ False

11. The music video for "Best Song Ever" was co-written by comedy star James Corden.
☐ True
☐ False

12. Harry says that when he eats a Twix bar he bites both fingers equally and simultaneously "to make sure neither of them gets lonely".
☐ True
☐ False

READY TO RUN

It's been another amazing year for Harry, Liam, Niall and Louis. In the studio and on tour across the globe, their hard work, talent and commitment have won them acclaim and admiration and, of course, the unswerving loyalty of their fans.

And having so many incredible experiences together has brought them even closer. Speaking of the other band members, Liam explains, "Saying that they are brothers to me is a bit of a cliché, but it's true. We are tied together by something special." Niall agrees. "They are genuinely the best guys."

As ever, it's all about the music. The boys share a passion for making great songs that are very much about who they are and how they feel. "We released our first albums when we were teenagers, so the lyrics and music reflected that period of our lives," Liam explains. "Now we are older and it's important both the music and lyrics reflect that." And Louis agrees. "We all feel that the music has really grown with us and our fans." Harry sums it up beautifully. "They're different stories being told in different ways."

In music and in life, whatever excitement the next chapter in the One Direction story brings, it's certain to be one you'll want to share with them every step of the way...

FROM US TO YOU

It's no secret that One Direction love their fans.

The lads have something to say directly to you...

Harry: It's very difficult to express just how important you are. We wouldn't be here if you weren't – you're everything!

Louis: I mean, how incredible are you?! You've just been so unbelievably supportive, creative, caring, passionate. I have so much respect and love for you and hope you love the new album this year.

Niall: You mean the world to us. This is surreal, and I am eternally grateful to each and every one of you who has supported us on this roller coaster. We are nothing without you.

Liam: You are the reason we have been able to have the life we have – we owe everything to you. 1D fans and the band are truly one. We are grateful for your unconditional support – eternally.